constructions

poems 1999-2011

kay sellers

Churchill Goodchild Poetry

G

Churchill Goodchild Poetry

Tumwater, Columbia, Cape Town

Sellers, Kay

constructions/Kay Sellers - 1st ed.

p. cm.

ISBN-13: 978-0-9836284-0-8
ISBN-10: 0983628408

Printed in the U.S.A.

constructions

poems 1999-2011

---

i am like a distracted child
who they drag by the hand
through the fiesta of the world
my eyes cling, sadly
to things...

~ juan ramón jiménez

modern[a]

- › modern
- › la moderna
- › late sketch(s)

modern
· · · · · · · · · ·

i

poem new year

winter appears palely,
there is a suggestion
of feathery powders

wind roughs the trees
strips the virtual air ..
the bend of the creek
cradles blocks of ice

what lies before us
are the trails thru
the shifting brambles
the graceful bones of grass
the crags in the symbolic hills
and the narrows of
bridges & ladders
under a skyward lazy eye

the measures of this day are
obscured by long thin sweeps
of clouds,, great extensions ..

these are agents
of a reborn year
heading for earth

ii

to(wards)

to get across town in twenty minutes is to move on against the grain of the traffic(s) .. it is the last day remaining of february,, there are crystals in the roads .. when i do appear,, i have a key to her house,, release ing the door .. we warmly will meet .. she does have the quality of a thinking animal .. i am too that paradoxic .. we together will make harmonic plans .. later defiant not skeptical,, on a crisp road to the reservoir,, we shall be walking up on the horizon ..

iii

sun(s)

what is your child made of(?)
.. is it from such a radiance
-- the sum of your smiles as
when the two you smile (?)

                    •

the sun will go a long way to you
it will slide down the sides
of the sky for you   and
across a plan of the earth to you
into your narrow room ..
the sun,, itself a soul,,
reveals that soul to the visionary

iv

(to the)1970 graduate

i know your fear,,
not in this ceremony
but in the times that will follow

all i can give is my faith &
my hands soft leather
to applaud you

i know you do not believe
in the power of your choices
yet you have well created me

so here is my life,, use it
draw upon it for asset
for the times that will follow

V

city black out

its neon city face has retreat d
and from that energetic face
its metallic communications
have ceased for now ..

the city is reduced to charcoals
while we huddle in the caves of our homes
around a scant flare of some sort of fire &
we wonder on & about ourself s

vi

thirtieth time

could it not be other than splashing smiles
and cymbals for now the thirtieth time (?)

we can not tell about how you will feel or
we know not upon what this might mean
but these are mystery s worth explore ing
on this the annual visit
,, a marker in the story
of your journey thru
the calender of existence

vii

modern

walking ::
scale,, character & significance are imposed ..

this particular place the avenue escapes north to infinity
so we cannot know the ancient ethers it leaps beyond to
but to the south
here is an end
at a new station
red red & yellow ..
a most concrete
post modern end

viii

jillian

i have recollect d her name
the impression she makes
.. what animates her
and her way of being

even i know now

she is present somewhere in a field of timelessness intoxicate ing on a moment

ix

miss lee

.. still she comes to mind
as once she was years ago
in the sierras near truckee
when she was flaxen & new
and again peering the firs,,
cirrus cirri & savage flowers
in ever the cold summery
morning(s)

X

linda

linda is in a state of kansas but she used to be here ..

somewhere in a vault is a moment that is construct d of her ..

tall as trees & as spare .. all arms legs with boy ish face ..

xi

anne marie

her face is much complex
as consequence of emotional surety

it is the summer of her years
the spring season is spent

observe her brow was pale now but has intricated   and
her voice has enrich d with the refinement of her thoughts

.. this all while she deepens with in to her life

xii

sal

again i am compell d to think
of myself thinking of her

our characters are strand d
on a divorced beach

this is a coda ..
it pulses with
memory s lost
in a scramble
of a half light of
a 1000 1000 yrs

xiii

boy

from a

re-

mote

after

noon

he

waits

the

bus

.. the tall dark boy nexts a long light pole

•

after that :: he walks with impersonal extensions for each arm *spring(s)*

the spring woman
in the television
is intent here ..

by contrast
she meekly points
to the swollen images
in our other states ..

she is back soon then
with prophetic fires &
with promised release

       •

spring the season   is
or
spring is   the season

for wind
seen here
in sienna
filters
and virga
rain shy
from
artistic
clouds

XV

in town

that gangly building in town on the town corner across of the presbyterians' church has a handsome soul .. an interior of ash grey faded pale

•

and what repair is this (?)

the strange trucks
in our street(s) ..
grinding
concrete
skin to
expose
municipal
nerves
and
muscle

•

a garden in the wall .. at the brick side tall entrance .. all so in town .. some thing might be said about the big mouth leaf s .. that greenly breath up the three story s of wall .. and that tremble,, a career,, in our presence

hwy 95

the south east shuffle of hwy 95 falls from reno & lake tahoe to the crimson valley

(and) nomadic high low ranch s be bless d .. their ginger prospects hurry the road

for fifteen miles or twenty miles visible spirits fall from wassuk range to walker lake

there are abyss s off parts of the road .. one wants not to imagine cuts in the earth

there are sinks/dry lakes,, out of sight,, miles miles long with body s of salts & soils

foreign buildings bleeding metallic & of a military distance moor some surroundings

the human constructs of boundary s are ignored by a boundary peak straddle ing 2 states

a generation of signs tempt the death valley west an hour & a detour to below sea level

the embitter d valley 'amargosa' never forgets,, it perseveres memory s in the land ..

while cactus springs & indian springs succeed the depressions of the low lands of las vegas

xvii

they

they place
behind the
mountains
in late
summer

they wait in the blue bricks

they can rise after the noon
in a chalk mild mood or
with in a state of rage

•

and what we can not see out of sight is
the monumental hand that is move ing

xviii

neighbor(s)

the neighbor sits
on steps stairs
out side above

she has a dim cigarette
one or two each day ..

and a shadow in her voice
if she wants to say hello

●

the persian neighbor who lives with his family in the east apartment
enjoys to smoke near the interior courtyard .. in the sun cold sunday

some seas

we go by a sea ..

the displaced seeking
an elusive residence ..

longing a hope
before liquid doors

·

yet off the coast
birds & beasts
have their
classical islands

no one human is allow d

·

and there is the marble fog on the

day beach

·

as well as the greater theatre ..

it lets
   rain
seaweed
stones

stones

XX

la jolla

at la jolla --
the streets
universally

under a tan sun

linen sidewalks
        fresh cars
roses green red
and rose voices

•

at the university,,
a beach for dawn

the sky so unfolds
the sand dunes
pose for flight

xxi

day(s)

some how i have
lost a gone day

i stand aside my self
or i am no use .. even
  next door some one
guilts a spent afternoon tuesday

                •

 today is twenty years of days ..

                    the city that chooses me
                    the sequence of beggars birds bells
                    the knowledge of what is lustrous
                            -- transitive though

will it continue with me
where ever I be &
when ever I am being(?)

xxii

regret

        friend of my ghost regret
        carry s an emotional stamp,,
        she who has been just recently by
        and has no want to leave yet

she who eternally inquires
about despair &
the long ago but
when i respond politely
she be comes anger d
now so too I am angry
then she does not care

◆

dear janet :

> *(oh) let me tell you,,*
>
> *they make rain in seattle*

ə

i think:

how long since

i have heard you ..

is the moon so virtuous

in seattle & are you

too devout

to your life

        or now do you walk down a street

        and the street becomes you

        then do you move as the bee

        on the whims of experience(?)

b

i think:

teach me

your speech

of spells ..

> they do induce drowsiness &
>
> vapors of the stocky chords
>
> from the bobbing sea   and

~

tell me again about water,

the disposition of lakes,

rivers, channels & bays ..

> how do you cross over &
>
> how is it that you change(?)

C

you think:

tides are, of course,

   a rhythmic rise & fall but the cause

   is an impelling attraction by sun

   by moon on earth & its waters

    ~

concerning rain bows ..

   they, yes, are a type of construction of color

   of light of sun reflecting on air bound waters

   suspended in arcs up beyond us

♩

you think:

water envelops us,

it is an element

of our atmosphere

> humidity measures the amount
>
> of water as vapor or a gas
>
> in a portion of air and
>
> vapors can become fluid
>
> influenced by an adjustment
>
> in temperature & an adjustment
>
> in saturation in a portion of air

e

i think:

it seems equally mystifying here

to see condensation streaked,

tan, orange sometimes yellow,

across the upper levels of sky

　　　　　.. many times though

　　　　　never to contact earth

ʃ

you think:

it is right to confuse

wind & current, these are

indeed movements of air

       though wind is the horizontal

       and current the vertical ..

       so then they are products

       of variances in pressure +

       the warm against the cool

       the light against the heavy

9

i think:

.. i understand,

climate realizes

it self in stages on the

olympic peninsula,

the land reflects on

its emotions above

    & driving from the straits,

    do you feel your feelings rise

    under the parental eye

    of mount olympus(?)

h

you think:

i dream

of a sky

in this certain color

        and now i am in it

        .. at shipyard' dusk,

        relative to southwest

        spokane street

        ~

or here in a post storm,

layers of atmosphere

above a bridge of possibilities,

        via an afternoon ..

        i motor affectively

        from west vancouver

        to the stanley park

i

i think:

the closeby planets

set at dawn ..

      and i envision

      a first light

      bounces up off

      the trampoline

      of the harbor

      and the inside

      of you leaps

j

you think:

is it for joy

that we persist(?)

        i walk/escape to a café

        ,, the out doors is wistful

        and i order a bright coffee

        then visualize myself,

        with you,

        a friend,

        a companion

        ,, who enjoys

        to imagine me

◆

i

she & i have
a spice worth
sharing ..

our kitchen flour

is snowing
on the floor

on the table
are vegetables
of many class s

grapes & berry s

are ready on
the counter

we are stoned
on the honey d
light

we
wear the
brothy eyes &

what can we do
with our recipe
of intimacy(?)

ii

we can create
an ideal of good,,
one that can be easy to affect

we muse ::
intimacy thrives on
healthy scaffolds

there is a
leafy ness to
our relate ing

what
we
afford

is patience
and barter d
emotion

we paint that emotion
,, give it a body
circle it in white

examine that body
in particles
of light

iii

in consonants
in deceptive vowels
there are virtual aspirations

the chameleon of
our afternoon hides
the red impulses

still we channel
across the
julieene distances

and the purple night
is lacerated by
our thoughts

we so
gather or
merge ..

we converge
to a common
theme &

become
content
editors

iv

for the heart
to be come
a bowl ..

the mind
must be
a bowl

notice the roundness
in the arms
of companions

is it how
we become
toss d(?)

then will
we own
sleepy arms &

will we wake
in the arms
of the future(?)

shall then we recall
what it is
that we are(?)

V

every sun rise
the forest holds
its breathe

there are no
churches here
only the supple land

and the trees
on this trail
are marry d

trail of loops..
one brings you away
one brings you back

a flask of clouds
nip across the
keen meadow

the sagging floor
is a carpet
of tremble ing ferns

and whiten rain,,
almost
snow

vi

what are
the octaves
of our lives(?)

what is its ethos,,
what is preserved(?)
and

are we who we are
with good reasons &
for good reasons(?)

year by year
a barn is fill d
& empty d (again)

inside the sky
there is a filtering
of pigments

the man on the plaza
enjoy s his burden ..
florals white yellow

and we are bound
even now by trains
green to the future

la moderna

~

quito moderno

en las alturas

hay goteras en las nubes,,

los aviones fuertes están nadando en el lago del aire

y las montañas continuan crecer ..

(¿) pero como me parece el paisaje urbano allá (?)

modern quito

in the heights

there are holes in the billows,,

strong jets swimming in the air' lake

and the mountains continue to grow ..

but how does it seem to me the cityscape (out) there (?)

~

i

how many flights of stairs to the moon
or at least to your house(?)

        the wind resists,, happy for a slight distraction
        and gravity knows it again will in the end win ..

        the bell in the gate
        the dog in the door
        the glass in the wall
        the protective man
            in the streets
            with his eyes
            with a gun &
               with a chain

then
so to you

ii

it is not very private.. even if you are forced to look at
the fair *pichincha*,, the mountain,, bathing in the last
of the evening' waves

●

once that *pichincha* lies down

~ see her recline ing face ~

silhouette.. glints with stars

from sky s & city s

iii

why would the rain bother with the coast(?)

in portly *manta*
,, the sea city,,
a cryptic feel

•

across the bridge to *playa tarqui*,, the beach
,, small fisherman with proud noses
prepare for journey
enjoy ing distances
for imprecise days

iv

newspapers say breakfast in *cuenca,,* the southern city,,
include ing papaya & oats costs *cincuenta centavos*

someone says wash day along the river
el río tomebamba is a spectacle

one child says the vocal dialect there is off beat
not a way of speaking but of singing

some people say all so that an angel protects the city
from domes the color blue above the cathedral

V

parade of sundays ..

the vendor & buyer
at the market in *parque el ejido*,,
the park,, know the expectations

•

the man who can not speak &
who walks from person to person,,
asks for favors with his broken paper

the man who can not walk &
the other with the twist d arm
accepts the care in the streets

vi

indigenous people
take what they will
tuesdays & thursdays
in this district,, *el batán*,,
unfolding refolding the trash sweetly

•

on the road to *nayón*,, an outskirt,, this the city dump is pick d thru by the many ..
and so what happens to the remains of a city(?)

•

or thief s live in houses with crows &
broken floors ..
they have what they have but want very more

vii

the rain in quito moderno,, the modern city,, is passive
never to disturb,, it does not have to travel for work far

•

the light in side rain is as a tone in side
autumn & more .. it is modest & metrical

•

the sky is a liar ..

these mornings the sun reforms easily as a grey disk ..

drunken men pee in the park & when the afternoon arrives they hide in be hind the rains

•

2 am / .. / rain fog / the wind is asleep / & / the sky has /a stolen face /

•

certain weightless days / .. / the precipitation of oracles / .. /not seen /-- / deep ly felt

viii

this world of white holes in & black holes out (tao) ..

•

then this day(s) in september there is a black hole over new york,, energy out,,

en parques,, the parks,, in *quito moderno,,* the brown pigeons small like doves

do not fly

•

¿donde está la abertura blanca? (or) where is the white hole(?)

•

I walk to want in down *avenida doce de octubre,,* the avenue,, next to the rains

with out a(ny) body

there is a ..
or there are breaks
in the inclemency s &
the sensation of clarity,, present in march
is the sun on its oval path inside celestial mechanics ..
perpendicular light .. then all then is most direct most apparent

•

or i could say ..

during weeks in march i am startled more than once by the attendance of light .. spring equinox imply s that the sun is overhead directly especially at the equator .. vertical light makes clear everything .. all surfaces are penetrated

X

el pan de ecuador
está en todas las partes ..
en las cuadras de la cuidad
y a veces en las manos de la gente

the bread of ecuador
is every where ..
in the city blocks
and at times in the hands of the people

•

and too there,, that store has a depiction of our suffering lord
near to a poster of a top less woman holding a can of motor oil ..
these are by way on the way to the bakery next door to buy moderate bread

xi

listen to the moon
sleeping this night
casting no shadows
in this gullible capital
with these cautious men
who can become pointless
with in these blind districts

       somewhere the gods
       in care of chaos
       are stupid
       with joy

      •

on the night side of the street
just out side a range of lights
.. the flourish of dark wings
      and darken body s

xii

is it certain,, what taxi drivers say that it could be dangerous there(?) ..

and but we go to the old market,, *san roque*,, in the old sector,,

quito antiquo below the avenge ing angel on *panecillo* hill

where we descend & descend far beyond the confident

           boundary s of the self

xiii

        if this city thinks off white ..
      so dust grows from building sites
ash descends from occasional volcano s
fumes ascend from producers
exhaust rises from vehicles
  chalk lifts from streets &
fog braids with smoke of
  near mountain blazes

when jets lose their way to *mariscal sucre* airport
possibly they will down in some sea green of parks

      •

and that field there is in love with the morning
.. the green morning with its suspension
and the children who are green
and sensationally defer d
in the morning
& the field

first week april
parque metropolitano
the metropolitan park
.. fog of floating sheets
with impressions of
trees in it   with
voices of children,,
laughing horses &
        flutes in it

XV

far miles away
the peak *cotopaxi*
pokes a hole in the sky
and smiles strongly upon
          carcelén,, the district,,

a woman with a wheelbarrow
fill d with sand is crossing the street

three men are carry ing cinderblocks
up & down ladders of an undress d building

a man drops long filaments of rebar off a roof
while another picks up & drags it down the street ..

and the children are nearby satisfy d with their plays of work xvi

i walk the avenues
october may june
            .. the drivers
in their vehicles are
flaw less musicians
staccato technique
as is accent d by
curses & car horns ..
a symphony
though atonal
performing by the
bright of the noon

                    •

and
dear beautiful chauffer ::
bus us thru speed limits
and thru needy red lights ..
it does not matter;; + surely
we ought to hurry in order
to arrive on time for those
parts of our lives that are
as yet so undetermined

xvii

en quito
si o no
(?)

it is ok for men to pee in the street
if their backs are turn d

bifocals allow you at
once two views

the street dogs will not attack you
if you walk beyond their territory

under some conditions may
$2 + 2 = 5$

the markets in old town in the day are less
dangerous than my street at night

a personal god is circular with a center everywhere
and a circumference no where

the negative ions in the here high streets
are not negative for us

light is a particle
and is a wave

there is no considerable change here from spring
to summer or fall

love is a particle
and is a wave

the first world must proceed from the second
and the second from the third world

→

the highs will be around 25°c & lows about 8°c & rain is likely
in the forecast for today & the following next year

my landlady makes $0.83 an
hour teaching english

this city has a mind that
is suspicious of itself

the sky above is construct d of
sheer fluids & blue crystals

only unexpectedly can one find the part of the place
in the park where bells lives

the bus to the middle of the
world costs $0.35 cents

no no,, no no,, yes
means may be

xviii

      in the dream ..
fear appears as a man
that you used to know

the man is waiting for
your contempt & for you
to tell him to go away

   •

       dear thick dreamer ::
there are fresh messages waiting
but you have to retrieve them
when it darks & after
you are peaceful

   •

then a night with courageous dreaming ..
the melodic sounds of galloping repeat &
the words *caballo caballo caballo* repeat
in side the brown muscles of your mind

xix

you are worthy
in & of yourself
though you try
to refute it

or today you wear
mists & eucalyptus ..
you smell of contrition

and so i want you for a gift
after noon or after vespers
though probably the former & as well to know
the all of you under the most transparent conditions

XX

is it dark(?)
or the other ..
that moment in
between day & dark

before the street lights light

the sky prepares to sleep in its
    bed of plums

the players move to the edge of
    the park

there is domestic desire among some
    but the popular bus s have stray d

there are beneficent beings in dark clothes
    among us who are prophetic

tengo dos dólares cincuenta,, una llave vieja,,
    una cinta,, una carta extrajera y una poema blanca
        en el bolsillo de la camisa

(or) i have two fifty,, an old key,, a ribbon,, a foreign card
    & a white poem in my shirt pocket

also the blind man walks as comfortably as us

those in love levitate freely think freely +
    articulate without constraints

bakery s empty & then restaurants fill

& my shadow turns to bear witness

this lyric between
the familiar & the new --
        or between risk & safety ..
quito is the risk but i have protection ..

the landlady has a dog to warn of robbers & a cat to warn of mice
an iron gate on the door & pretty bars in the inside of windows
.. a friend suggests fresh flowers in the kitchen
or another advises me to burn white sage
and too there is my fallen angel
who enjoys to follow me

                .

it is the verb of evening &
the moon has fallen among
the tallest trees

.. i follow myself into the body of the city
or is it (?) my angel & i following me
into the dark artery s of quito

◆

23 dec – quito

i leave in a taxi.. almost one o'clock., am . with two bags .. why is it not raining (?) .. this is quito after all .. the driver has no meter so i know i will be charged too much.. i am just who i am .. but how much am i worth (?) ..

•

there are always people waiting outside this airport .. only passengers allow d in .. to pass thru an expectant crowd is a unique joy .. maybe they are passing some of their expectancy on to me .. the airport in quito is unimpressive & airless but there is salsa music on the speakers & the monitors .. later the plane fly s to guayaquil then lima ..

•

guayaquil
guayaquil from the air
horizontal with
many suntan d artery s of water ..

in the deep channels
.. barges very large

•

it is the third day of winter in ecuador but of summer in perú ..

•

-two-

23 dec – lima / miraflores

lima

this is a city of 8 000 000

and at least the sectors

seem to me that i see are

of order & orderliness .. &

a/the driver weaves in & out

of streets near the pacific ..

the air is a warm lotion

and of the sea ..

•

23 dec – cusco

cusco has a feel of small buildings brown with reddish tile roofs .. a rural feel,, reddish dirt .. the old sector is well & true colonial coexisting with inka roots .. some of the streets are so narrow i can stretch both arms to touch almost the sides .. the school for language,, my host family' home,, the main plaza are all on or near avenida el sol .. i am met at the airport by a member of the family ..

.. i will for two weeks have simple meals & a room -- a bed,, a chair,, a table for to write for to read & a window to cusco .. what more is there (?) ..

•

24 dec – cusco

i have come to believe that spanish is the native language of the world .. i am fluent in a foreign language,, english,, & inadequate in this continent' native language .. language is acquired thru immersion,, in dialogue & in culture .. the practice & study of another language is assembled in the mind,, that non physical space,, & the mind assembles pieces like a puzzle except that it can place pieces in non interlocking locations ..

•

25 dec – cusco

the family wakes me for midnight .. christmas is celebrated like new years,, fireworks & shouts .. christmas dinner at 1.20 o'clock, am ..

•

less police & soldier presence in perú .. the people are poorer here .. indigenous people some with out shoes ..

•

dark
está escondiendose el tarde
globos brillantes en los montes
en noche, los filos
(or)

-four-

the afternoon hides itself

bright globes in the foothills

edges in the night

26 dec – cusco

there is a big soccer game between lima & cusco .. cusco has lost .. as i walk down a long way from downtown & the plaza,, hordes of young men,, disappoint d & drinking,, are walking up a long way to the downtown & the plaza .. on the sideways in the streets & follow d by,, in full riot gear,, dozens of police

•

27 dec – cusco

i am make ing a list of things i forgot, to bring ..

•

on avenida el sol near the plaza,, money changers on the streets .. soles to dollars or dollars to soles .. largess hands full of money s ..

•

28 dec – cusco

on this street is a man playing harmonica with no hands for use .. his harmonica is placed between the lower parts of his arms .. he works he has friends & family,, he is fed & cared for .. is that enough (?)

•

-five-

statue

la luna llena .. el cristo blanco,, los brazos extendidos

está adentro de los cerros la estatua lustre ..

(or)

the moon .. cristo blanco,, arms are extend d

polish d statue in side the hills ..

•

     29 dec / 30 dec – aguas calientes / machupicchu

this train zigzags thru the inclined city .. cross s & other totems on rooftops,, flash by .. then a four hours, from cusco to aguas calientes & machupicchu above .. the landscape during the train trip is fertile & ancient,, guard d by towers of mountains ..

•

machupicchu

city of old terraces ..

the ruins the double rainbow

then jungle & tan river below

there seems equivalent mountains

    their peaks pierce ing the sky

→

-six-

bring rural rain
the god of sun
inka time
and choice
to disappear

•

     31 dec - cusco

last day of the year .. i sleep only to wake to sleepwalk in the city ..

•

new years eve
to raise with others
perhaps a few 30 000
in the plaza de armas

with in a fired moment
lift d as between years

•

     01 jan – cusco

i take a trip to the ruins,, sacsayhuamán,, above the city .. a public
park to the citizens of cusco who picnick,, play soccer & laugh among
centurys' old stones .. first day of the year ..

•

02 jan – cusco

earth

la tierra llena .. (¿) cuales son las memorias

y cuales ha disculpado(?)

(or)

flush earth .. what are your memory s

and what have you forgiven (?)

03 jan – cusco

of the too many museums in cusco .. there is an unusual one,, of inka,, it is located in a large building with an interior patio separating in one part of the building,, a modern bank for finance,, while in the other part a museum to the spirit & past of the inkas ..

•

04 jan – cusco

i see to a shaman today,, near the small plaza san blas,, he says my soul has questions for me to answer ..

•

05 jan – cusco

is this nearly my final day is this infinite city(?) .. i walk to the market near & near the train station ..

•

06 jan – cusco & above perú

i realize i do not even know the name of the street that i have lived on for
two weeks .. all i know is that it is near avenida el sol ..

•

taxi early to a cusco airport .. we believe we are the only ones on these roads ..

•

clouds

this ship fly s within the levels of them

mountains peek their spike heads thru them

below them are the contour d body s of the world

then & the sea,, a wrinkled mirror reflects them

•

jetplane

desde el avión entre cuzco y lima

hay las paredes de montañas,,gris/oliva

con muchos lagos, abajo de las cimas blancas ..

lagos de hielos verdes ..

(or)

from the plane between cusco & lima

there are walls of mountains ,, grey/olive

     with many lakes below the peaks white

          lakes of green ice ..

•

    06 jan – quito

the taxi driver has no meter .. i know i will be charged too much ..

it wants to rain ..

•

◆

1

    showers are a constant ..

    water rings out in streets/sidewalks

    down the sides of buildings

    in this particular city

2

    when the sun appears ..

    no warmth

    though it is reflect d

    from a million mirrors

3

    there are sharp concave

    & convex shapes

    onto certain brick d

    residential streets

4

    and even temper d

    people are dress d

    as dark

    flowers

5

and bus s & taxis

shake thru

the channels

of streets

6

underneath

the subway is a snake ..

it stops to ingest

everyone

7

or else the whole city

can vibrate,,

4 or 5 seconds

a little tremor ..

8

and is there a vague mist

inside & outside

that

mystify s (?)

9

and why are the
church bells
following
me(?)

10

and how is it,, at night
do buildings stately
thicken .. take on
a different life(?)

11

. . also i consider there are
mountains in the east
that half fill the
andean sky

12

and the evening view
from above .. these
blue & white mountains
are sunk in sun rinsed clouds

13

now a real defined spring

commences ..

tentative blossoms

opposite french doors

14

regardless :: vendors of empanadas

want to cure

your hunger

for 100 pesos

15

.. persistent gypsy s

want to cure

your soul

for 100 pesos

16

while street vendors of books

want to sell you

used wisdom

for just little more

17

    or hallwalks

    in the university s

    .. everyone is eager

    but what for(?)

18

    then – near by there,,

    exists a solid formality

    of rows of houses ..

    though there are exemptions

19

    as what of that house (?)

    here near a corner ..

    nearly

    airborne

20

    and the street

    that it lives on ..

    nearly

    lifting

21

    now i am in the air

    in a bridge

    over a street

    connecting two different worlds

22

    in one world ..

    count the images of the dictator

    every where that

    never seem to fade

23

    otherwise .. a corona of frustration

    via civic protestations

    ripple thru

    the city

24

    and

    ripple thru

    the narrow expanses

    transverse ing this country

25

.. between that expanse
of the mountains
of the coast .. is a
metaphysical friction

26

or does the oppositions
in the southern cross
out up there .. suggest
in down here – contention(s)

27

meanwhile the highway becomes us
thru valleys
hills & tunnels
then this abrupt coast

28

there you might find
one more city .. (this one)
symbiotic in its hills above
the shores

29

    seafood & advice

    here are rich

    while modernism

    is misplaced

30

    .. but placed

    at the edge of a beach,,

    buoys & stars are speaking freely

    yet abandon d in the evening

31

    and fishermen throw

    their netting flat

    in to

    the sea

32

    as poets throw

    their verse blank

    in to that

    similar sea

33

these (all) are drown d

to be later

surfaced

& emotional

34

and unknown somehow

a boon of sparks

are turn d in on &

on in a pacific bay

◆

i

if she had turn d left instead of right

that one day long ago in valparaíso de chile,,

she would now be there on the coast &

probably live ing in a funky place in the hills

over down town that faced the bay that faced

the sea but & she would she would be working

in a small university in that area & also spending

a lot of time at her friend' good place,, a place

that would have slight strips of paper suspend d

from invisible wires near the ceiling,, papers

that contain d illuminate ing verse ..

ii

if she had a cup of coffee instead of tea many
years hence in the bay area of the usa then she
might still be there but live ing in oakland of
california near the stadium in order to have an
occasional experience of some magnitude +
also undoubtedly she would be working be working
in a small private school in berkeley of california
& spending a lot of time at an artist friend best
friend' house that would have completely bare
walls except for very small calligraphy depictions
in those walls in most every room of the house ..

iii

she should have taken the subway not the bus that
one certain day, en la cuidad de mexico, the city of
mexico because she could be there now & she would
likely be studying the new testament & mostly the
pauline letters at a little philosophical seminary plus
live ing near it,, en la zona rosa,, with a newly made
friend whom she could be very interest d in & who also
would have a car that she could borrow during future weeks ..

iv

maybe instead of lunch in april on a thursday

three years from now,, she could consider

relocate ing to seattle of washington state

in where she could certainly teach for a tiny

state university & clearly take walks long in

the moisture & soft vapors soft vapors every day

with her future friend & they would definitely

live in a space near the harbor & it would

probably be fill d with constant watery reflections ..

V

if she had decided to go to paris of france
instead of not going a number of years ago
then surely she would be live ing there pre
sently + in le quartier latin ,, yeah the trendy
latin quarter,, & teaching without doubt at an
obscure academy,, but so like probably her french
would be terrible by parisian standards however
her writer friend would help her linguistically while
they would walk would walk those many of paris river bridges..

she might be in madrid de españa right now
if she had gone to europe long ago as she
had want d to or more specifically she could
be live ing in an old sector of the city in a
monk-like cell & could be studying medieval
texts of christian & islamic scholars during
the week while only on the weekends,, with
her crosstown friend,, she would travel south
to see respect d church s & mosques ..

she could have stay d in lima de perú some

time ago but she did not though if she had

she might be with in a shortwalk of the pacific

from a condo in miraflores & she could probably

teach at a quiet international college + definitely

she would be destined to meet a very interesting

university friend at a serene sidewalk table

over coffee over coffee & periodicals ..

(or)

she might have been in são paulo de brasil

if she had not linger d that day in rio de

janeiro de brasil & likely she could be teach

ing in a vibrant small prep school plus of course

she may live in a small really quite expensive studio

by somewhere near somewhere near avenida paulista

and obviously she would struggle with the language

of portuguese but she would luckily receive help

from a soon to be friend & also they both probably

will surely delight each other with probability(s) ..

i

sparrows see souls as they fall thru ex
explode ing clouds to new born body s

she could break her arm when she
follows the sun thru that window

an old california mission with saint rooms up
down with the beatific sea at the back lawn

someone told me,, those stones small secret
in her portable pockets,, are from the africas

i guess the airport in albuquerque is the near est
place but brief,, to lift up away off from the earth

across the street some one
opens second story curtains

the sky could hurt you
if only you will let it

sun filters thru & thru
the cottonwoods

after crossing the border
the ivory sky will ignite

and should i mail you a
packet of round light(?)

ships too far out in the sea still know
of & that there are waiting harbors

from a dream i see her reading so i wake myself
and make a black tea for her & re turn to sleep

she stubborns as a left hand d
girl in a right hand d world

crush resin crystals,, marry lime & turpentines
choose true hues -- raw umber,, ochres & sienna

so what wind would howl down the
street&not want to rush our lives(?)

she can feel the ocean
any time she wants to

in her favorite jersey & jeans she
gent ly levitates about the room

she has curves like the ones
in the road to her house

he drives -- she looks
at the side of his face

so a bouyant book is im
impatient to be touch d

iii

no one could survive in half moon country
with out being disfigured by its beauty

debussy pleases you -- you are
drawn to the waves in his music

yesterday walking by the neighbor' open
window,, a piano play d (richard) strauss

they lie vertical in air,, miles above the
ground to hammer in the white stones

the road to their house is like blood
soft dirt,, this time of late summer

there are deep wrinkles
in those mountains near

you play prokofiev in side
as children play tag out side

a morning street :: smells lilac & dwarf
pine,, looks lavender & burnt lime

her hands folding & unfolding --
such tulips (!),, waxy vivid&vivid

she says she works for
the ministry of beauty

beverly lives in vestments & delivers
the persimmon word to cloudy people

jo (ann) is maroon d in
the island of los angeles

rose lives beneath her personal mount
ains that are beneath the green d sea

colleen wakes & the
valley wakes .. too

in an earthbox,, jessie keeps her voice & in an
air box,, her thoughts & in a firebox,, her hearts

karyn' hair is sweet ropes
bind d by the historical rings

(and) now she is gone,, anne marie --
who has sail d for maine in a sluggish car

journal .. marta impress s her life in one,,
dayxday .. in september she drew in trees

fionna teach s the
art of polishing air

pearl teach s the
art of preserving icons

V

is there no defense against
the theology of spring(?)

fire off along the road but only a few will stop
to see the work of a meso american god un fold

the fisher king' coma
expires .. charity returns

the dog next door looks at the world
thru its huge eyes & gathers sorrow

was it 1963 that a too human
president became mythic(?)

the person in that pretty box
only used to be friend larry

jeff .. he still carry s the spear & the
shields but the heavenly wars are over

is not it true -- when drive ing thru the
mojave the road turns ruby d(?)

muffled morning -- man &
motorcycle muscle mainstreet

now billows poach d with im
impossible quality s,, sail(eth) west.

§

[dis]order

> if we go outside

> a night of dreams

> she is in indigo

> 13th may .. leave

> the train station

i

if we go outside then it would be the first day of the year or a day that is very close to our past ..

rust tones & ash ones & pine ones blow in from four directions .. the sky allows light, curtails of light .. the air cracks, sharply frequently, and ripples .. there are the just realized ancient hills, easy hill trees, diminished hilly brush, defensible hilltops & implied foothills beyond.. but released of these scenes our standing petitions seem to wander with ease as weightless as chaotic birds, without hesitancy(s) .. no obstacles ..

ii

in the middle of an afternoon, a white blue afternoon, a cloud has covered the sun and we could not have expected the subsequent emptiness or pure state of absence .. of the ever present channels around us, the ones used for the passage of sound and the displacement of air, from one location to another, these are stopped but momentarily .. suddenly this day has stopped, though momentarily ..

however what we can understand and visibly, are the smooth undercurrents of the organism that is our town, how one of many actions begin as others end, and how multiple purposes and diverse reactions complement each other; these are now noticeable but only momentarily ..

iii

as unpredictable as a day in march can be, there are riches in its surprises .. each day is noticeably a distinct length and the width of its moods are represented by the weather ..

no one is more at home at this time than these two cats who simultaneously notice & disregard everything .. they are serenely awake .. and for each season of the calendar, they are renamed, the cats, and they seem to continue to respond to their new labels.. one morning, it began, the morning began wintry, with cats in attendance, and with a heavy curtain of shadow that presaged the arrival of a storm .. two days later all evidence of that event was gone; and the cats were balanced on window seats calmly attentive to the introduction of a new day ..

one afternoon in march they played with light falling into a room and then later that afternoon they tormented some hapless creature .. somehow, both events displayed equal grace ..

when the hour shifts artificially, one hour forward in the spring and one hour back in autumn, is there a container of time that is moved from one space to another(?) .. we do know that the natural cycles of spring exists and the autumn .. but what is it that is carried, as real time, that is continually displaced and ceaselessly replaced(?) ..

we do know that motion, even thru time, suggests change and change implies, thru our minutes days years, implies existence and our part or participation in that existence ..

V

mid-year, everyone observes conventions .. traffic flow is explicable; pedestrians walk predictably, except for events downtown, that are solely for the visitors and unrestrained children .. some suppose that the actions of these days are mild; the trees make little sound as they rustle; automobiles brake respectfully; winning teams are not extravagant; the grazing winds are brief refreshment; and insects live short but fulfilling though not annoying lives ..

the practice of the content, the contented, is the harmony inherent in active routine; the careful cultivation of principle; timely shops and street vendors that begin each day with constancy; and the people speaking, their desires, each night, into the reasonable night ..

vi

further south, remote from here, and at a different period of time, we walk to a river thru serviceable paths .. lean canals are greened with moss & algae .. we enter a wood of large unsentimental trees, cottonwoods, and fallen branches that are mixed among willowy brush .. it is a reduced day and we encounter studied walkers, children with careful dogs and practiced riders on horses .. we collect flat, easy to grasp stones .. we walk to a sandy bank .. the river flows seamless though it does wrinkle, at times, with a subtle watery ripple or airy ripple .. the light folds into portions of the river .. across the river, the shore has foliage that has been restrained by the season ..

it is a condensed day and we are enticed to release past, unused, reminiscence of other, distant, collections of water in order to experience this fresh one, this new river ..

it is the walking, someplace nearby, that brings the land, our terrain, into scale and it is the immersion into the rudiments of wind, thickness & wetness of atmosphere and the sensation of foot in shoe and shoe on uneven surface that makes us part of it ..

we want to hear the sounds of the person striding next to us, the rustle of their clothes, and the cadence of their step, and the changing quality of illumination on their moving figure and the mixed unique pitch of their tone of voice .. we speak common words though these are partially erased at times by the setting that may have some occasional dull distant deliberate unrecognized roar ..

in the background, unseen planes could be starting & stopping, midair, somewhere and someplace that is nearby ..

water diminishing on a path is endemic of the reiteration for discreet movement in an arid place ..

we hike in the evenings, after the sun has set, because the remaining minutes of fading luminescence are temporal & safe .. the regular wind truncates speech so we make hand signals and knock elbows .. the up and down shift of the blush hills make us appear stationary, the crunch of small rocks and their sharp ricochet, the brush of bush of trees against the fabric of our clothing, locate us concretely in a particular peculiar location in space that is just beyond the backyards of neighbors' homes houses ..

from another perspective, helicopters patrolling, distant, appear stationary ..

construction zones in the south, south of town, extend to the north .. and she stands in her parking lane to imagine a route before she drives it .. many automobiles navigate yet their drivers are only sometimes mindful of this automatic practice but the ability, capability, of her car is printed on her mind .. the few accidents, in the town, that do occur are out of necessity, rarely randomized, to vividly manifest some larger design ..

she sees the wind on the window, the window of the car, she is softly attentive and anticipates the next turns ..

X

dust devils, dust storms in miniature or dry land-bound tornadoes in miniature, form on the sides of isolated roads, in the height of the day, seemingly at random .. our dispositions are braced for unexpected disturbances .. yet on sunny & steady days, for a moment, the sudden updraft of air, touches ground creating a swirl, a swirl of dirt of dust and sound ..

yet, though, our dispositions are braced for unexpected turbulences ..

xi

at night we could dream of oceans, surrounding waves, the inability to stand, inaccurate touch, soggy speech and loss of audio precision & loss of balance .. when awake, at day, in the persistent light of summer, we convince ourselves of no such matters and imagine waves that would morph into grasses .. then we could travel to the land where there are such foaming grasses ..

on foot into desert high desert meadows, we are silently alert, with pastures at the knees; and there, and there are physical waves to be touched ..

the soil between our hands, which we had to buy to integrate with the uncooperative top soil of our high desert, has a cool temperature, a muscular musk and consists of silky clumps .. in exchange for the simple planting of native grasses and the strategic placement of rocks and of ground cover, we ache in new ways ..

and we connect; yet how, we cannot understand, yet we connect and in new ways ..

the statement - *we walk into the civic square, into the full evening* - has had to come from somewhere, probably on or after an experience of an actual event of civic walking ..

so, if following the remnants of the sun, we walk into the municipal evening in the downtown or maybe the municipal twilight in the center of town; then we do notice booths and chairs and police in waiting, and the tall position of buildings .. and there are complete trees that move about, side to side, while remaining in place; and there is sound, disguised as words, bouncing between people in motion ..

we occasionally bump bodily, into each other, obviously along some uneven streets, in order to adjust, and readjust, the pace and tempo of our combined experience of a valid true public walk ..

this station, a terminal of seeming timelessness, is bittersweet because it is not a location that anyone can stay for long .. we are surrounded by numerous times and multiple continents .. all interior signs; markers, game plans, offers, intuitions; point to elsewhere .. transports arrive and depart, and depart quickly .. and we can sit or pause for an hour, for a thousand brief hours, but everyone eventually, before long, moves on ..

we are surrounded by numerous decisions and multiple outcomes .. although .. it is fortunate that we have this fleeting feverish moment, bittersweet; this moment of each other, for each other; in this awkward dislocated place, as we do soon pass on to elsewhere ..

XV

at the end, at the end of summer, it is supposed to rain or pretend to, in the afternoon .. the pretense, sly virga, is curved wind moist, the localization of color, and streams of light that evaporates in higher layers of sky; unlike real rain which bounces, once hitting ground, bruising the body and the mind ..

today we; having disappeared into a face of a real storm, and having lain down to make a containment or make a pool of our bodies; do emerge much weathered, much renewed ..

◆

a night of dreams

i

a night of
dreams
disordered,
therefore
a waking life
holds no surprises
.. but soon the
body flows
and the mind
recovers,

dreams improve ..
images of hopeful
medicines .. & an
 order of friends

ii

an order
of friends;
fluent from
inside to
outside of a
known house,
engaged in
a leafy
conversation ..

and it would be
the middle period
of several months
and the hours
would be
rich --
 would be
attentive

iii

the distance
changes,
between
the house
and the road,
every time
it is walked
.. alterations
in a plan by
the intent of
a greeting or

a turn of mood
by a newspaper
notification
or a turn
of feeling
thru a personal
          letter

iv

a driver
is lopsided
in a faded
vehicle ..
detained &
content
in the wake
of the weather

.. mild
in the 70s,
slightly damp
(spell) d,a,m,p
and currently
low incidences
        of discord

V

certain
houses
do occur in
this valley
because
they support
the grid
of accord
maintained by
green margins,

lank structures,
communal standards
and native markers,
and silent passages

vi

all
the absences
possible are
suggested above,
a semicircle
is lucid (spell)
l,u,c,i,d but
void .. shadows
are not visible

.. later a block
of wind rubs
against a block
        of clouds

vii

the perspective
of an afternoon,
diagonal,
enters
rooms ..

there
it is
a lean
(spell)
l,e,a,n
then an
orchestrated
      advantage

viii

there is a hole
in the afternoon,
mute colors
low colors
fall thru it ..
a plain hole
or a tear
in the afternoon ..
now, where we walk
little inconveniences
are scattered
among the lawn

now, when we walk
little disturbances
  are sprinkled
among the grass

ix

the dark falls
      on us ..
temporarily
dissipating
the day heat &
the day light

we count more
than 1000 (count)
1, 0, 0, 0
bright-nesses
among the spiral
planets the spiral
stars and the circle
      of the moon

X

buildings,
at darkness,
seem near us
at the perspective
of a roof top ..
and so, their
scale becomes
imaginable ..

but still
ignored,
other starry
black sights,
unknown astros
(spell)
a, s, t, r, o, s
& almost
forgotten,
planet(ary)
         motion

xi

thru the air
the rhythm,
we sense,
is the sound
of workers
talking
purposeful
and securely
into the houses
of the future

and they, then,
seizing them,
these constructions,
by hand
by steamy machine,
        seize them
    into existence

xii

the past
experience
of streets
is partially
abbreviated on
street signs ..
on the corners
there are small
angular codes ..

these are symbols
of overlapping
memories that are
modestly notated or
    cautiously stated

xiii

in description
of the lift off
of birds:
dispersion
into
a natural
symmetry ..

they drive
thru holes
in thru the
shifty air
until,
at rest, they
perch (spell)
p,e,r,c,h
invisible(ly)
    and rigid

xiv

houses in new subdivisions
adorn the outside of towns
.. episodes of renewal
as parcels of land
are seemingly tamed

but imperceptibly
the high desert
edges back ..
skews events &
 disrupts time

XV

we follow a clear panel
thru the atmosphere
until it evades us ..
but before we lose it,
vapored supports,
impressionable fabric
and inaudible music
            are revealed

.. reducing us
to ambiguity,
   engaging us
to be present

◆

i

she is in indigo clothes, has skin stained with the early hours of the day, has hair folded on her shoulders as a building opens to her & she hurries to walk to it .. or a very tall man of brown black skin brushed with grey, in a business suit, sees the environment parts as he walks, his hair long slightly .. or a simply tall woman wearing a purple suit made for her body & she with snowy skin, runs as the atmosphere gives, has eyes that pierce .. or she, who walks long stairs of public houses, has a dark face of dark orange ..

ii

he, with arms of a laborer, eyes heavy, copper & brass in his skin & is walking on side walks that concede .. or a woman of amber skin tones who glides in a river of streets, occupied with her books, briefcase & a flooded mind .. or a woman & a man, they have created a skin between them of electric colors, for example heightened, they notice parks narrowing & how when they both embrace they emit presence & radiantly .. or girls the color of hummingbirds, are armed with books & fidelity, fly thru stretched hallways of not small schools ..

iii

she is red & orange, and in the foreground are street noises that move to the background, as she busies her self thru concrete obstacles .. or children who are illuminated, their splendid colored faces swimming against a celebratory tide of twilight pavements while multi-flash of artificial fires is overhead.. or blued skaters, lightly weighted with snow, on clothes, skate & laugh across an iced lake .. or with a handful of stems & stalks, roots & seeds in pockets, a coffee-toned person comes & browses & goes again goes again goes again thru stalls of an open market ..

other blue skaters circle another body of ice, heavy knapsacks on arched backs, they do consider the effects of slant & velocity .. or yellow gardeners, burdened with garden dynamics & soil chemistry, do consider the rows of squash & of young cabbages .. or steel gray walkers, who do consider the labor of offices, are waiting for the change of a day, the change of a season a season a season .. or spring butterflies, spring colored, who are unencumbered, gliding thru rows of air .. or winter birds, winter colored, who are encumbered, on their mission from the north to the south ..

V

singers with citrus complexions, for example heightened, songs in their heads, hurry thin corridors onto spacious stages .. or the camouflage complexions of new soldiers struggling thru the mud in training fields .. or animal spotted people who have primitive tools & who stand in religious stillness in a rainforest .. or painted porcelain faces of actors actresses, in period clothing, who nervously wait to enter into the action of a play .. or on a beach, two friends, walking tightly, two friends of watery appearance, white blue appearance, who unhurriedly unburden their thoughts ..

vi

he, who is more charcoal than a grey skin, a boy of school age who takes a short cut carefully in a field of shards with a back bag of books .. or rust hues in a man, not short, who with large art canvas in hand, is waiting to cross a dizzy street .. or a woman with lunar skin, who has daily insights, for example heightened, parks a car & walks thoughtfully .. or, and/or, teenagers, carelessly loitering, with sandy & pink faces, faces reflecting faces reflecting faces reflecting in a window, faces stained with the late hours of the day ..

◆

i

13th may .. leave home from

      here new mexico @ 8:00 am
530 miles .. stop in

      gallup for gas .. extra windy
           washed landscapes transform deeply

      flagstaff to kingman .. large scenes

try/to relive/memories/of other roads ..

truckstop   near kingman .. yellow empty roads

      amber ones ..   burnt elevated ones

.. get a night room

ii

        leave for los angeles &

      less gusts today .. 14th may..
277 miles of

      circular atmosphere .. foaming heard

          112 degrees

in the mojave to barstow &   to san bernadino,

            drive is swift then athletic ..
          accurate directions to a friend ..

      partly blush ambiance ..

           a house a yard green

iii

absolute morning ..
travel san bernadino county   & los angeles county ..

touring mileage ..   hills made of houses

see movie see pool & garden green,

massive lunch   with friends .. stimulus scenes ..

later, sunset blvd ..
night hours   lateral ones

undivided ones

15th may

with drawn darkly scenes

iv

                              ritual goodbye to san bernadino

arrive to newport beach ..
              ought to get lost

      in huntington beach ..   dissonant scenes

16th may & coffee ..   303 miles ..

                      do passage to san luis
            via santa barbara ..

        copper like seas ..   golden ones
bronze like ones

      late/friends/dinner

V

thin like black aerial boundaries sharp ..
      17th may, ardent morro bay

   & locales ..

     pismo beach, sunken ..
          sane town/university/san luis ..

      exploring mileage ..   narrow threads of stairs

      to opaque coves in oso park ..
the seas are spinning

   island in a bay

for a million birds
      & notice surf .. washed scenes

vi

precise goodbye to san luis ..

    drive north,   odor rich of soil & growth

in the central valley .. farms, many workers work

    hwy 101 ribbons to san francisco ..
        violet 18th may,

a bluish one
        a serious purple one

    heavy traffic/in the city/sideways ..

arias of the walking people ..   marin then oakland ..

      jammed scenes ..
today 382 miles .. sacramento   in shadows

vii

leave sacramento 19th may..

perhaps 610 miles ..

abrupt slow mountains ..

find a heavenly valley in tahoe ..

to las vegas zigzag from reno ..

speckled & sacral terrain ..

highway collapses near las vegas ..

circus scenes,   rent room

viii

leave early las vegas ..

sun mirrors hoover dam ..

20th may .. distilled scenes

desert is a red photograph ..

a scarlet one ..
a cardinal one ..

the conic rise of flagstaff

from the landscape ..

639 miles to home

here, new mexico .. tangible scenes

◆

1

the train station and the bus station, in the city, westside & downtown, are within sight of each other, as is the main post office facility. dominant is the train station, regal with its towers and its classical american interiors.

every day and every hour, this area is overlapped with departures for all points in the city.

2

the imposing statue, on fifth avenue, is difficult to locate unless you are looking up. it is several stories above street level, crouched on a ledge in front of and incongruous with a post modern skyscraper. bus patrons waiting for numbered buses often look up at the statue looking down.

if the statue would stand up, it would be over fifty feet tall and could leave its perch, in order to walk clumsily down fifth avenue.

3

there is a rapid route through the northwest industrial sector. the traffic lights are few and synchronized although it is worthwhile to slow down and observe the surroundings. on the west side are the wooded hills of forest park and on the east side of this route are massive factories and ribbons of railway lines. all of this industry is squeezed next to the river, with its barges & giant cranes.

the periodic bridges lead across the river to other industrialized areas or sometimes to lush residential bluffs. most bridges are muscular and utilitarian but there are exceptions. sometimes a bridge that serves buses, cars and factory transports can be slender and lyric.

4

the university, that is south of st. john's community, is bounded by bluffs near the river. roads into and inside the school are thin and tight, probably to allow more room for the spacious lawns and the aggressive trees. students move reverently between classes. there are no apparent clocks.

students could spend free periods imagining the perceived distance between the bluffs and the river.

5

forest park stretches from the residential west hills neighborhood to the north, parallel to the river. there are vertical roads and precarious housing but these are outnumbered by the tall trees.

after dark, the radio towers on skyline drive are the only beacons in the big green night.

6

the light rail train from the airport to downtown is usually swift though it is not necessarily direct. it does offer an opportunity to see the city, unadorned and occasionally self-conscious. patrons, who do sit backwards while moving forward, can become confused about the nature of motion and direction.

the dividend of arriving at a destination, is pretending that it is for the first time and savoring the sensation of arrival.

7

for nine or ten blocks, the street connections between hawthorne blvd and its parallel sister, division street; collapse into ladd's circle. the streets here are diagonal and carefully overgrown within configurations of nature green. the street names are botanical; the elementary school resides on orange avenue.

the homes are recessed from the streets, a stage within the levels of green.

8

when it rains without cease for several days or several weeks, the city continues; traffic flows and people work. rain is a type of harmonics that is understood here. it is musical notes that can occur at a rate of 1000s of beats per second.

in pioneer square, people stroll on water concrete. the trains float on water rails.

9

it is possible to look straight into the ballpark stadium, from its 18th avenue side, although it may be difficult to understand what is going on. however the cheers of approval or groans of disbelief are recognizable. the frequent rains can be a source of exhilaration or despair depending upon the outcome of the games.

the newspaper plant and offices are nearby; they understand and market the currents of exhilaration and despair.

10

once a month, on a thursday, the people of alberta street are on display as much as their products. it is a carnival of personal industry and ageless vitality. many buildings are in stages of renovation and though others remain as they have for decades.

vendors sell clothing, local art and homemade food. street clowns entertain. spiritualists tell the future with only a small deck of cards or with a brief look at an open hand.

11

near a downtown church, a wedding party spill over the sidewalk onto 9th avenue as they walk from the church to an expectant restaurant for a reception. the slender south park blocks are hushed on a sunday morning. a few people reading newspapers, drinking coffee on the park benches. several transients asking for change.

the trees are so tall here, a canopy, that it is hard to notice the reliable rain.

12

the lean north park blocks have commercial and residential interests surrounding it. walkers with their dogs, readers with newspapers, transients, joggers and coffee drinkers collide.

13

someone whispers a word. it could be someone enthusiastic and waiting for a bus on martin luther king jr blvd, at a few blocks from the lloyd center. this word becomes a component of a fresh formless moment.

that moment might manifest as part of the experience of a couple walking south in riverside park near the ross island bridge.

14

the air here has a taste & texture that is augmented by the immediate surroundings. near parts of the river, the air is augmented by earthy water and the metallic tang of bridges, cars, trains, riverside factories.

on the west side of the river, north of burnside, home to quieted homes, the air has a nuanced austere additive.

15

it is indiscernible, the transition from the massive public buildings on the south park blocks onto the massive ones on the university campus. there are more people here walking everywhere and in the air, the sound of sporting events or musical events.

thru the windows of millar library, which are several stories & concave, there is the discreet sound of people reading & people thinking.

16

washington park, in the hills off west burnside, is a series of parks, gardens & natural destinations. cars & school buses crowd the curvy streets here and the light rail stop is underground. there are acres of wild forest and steep hillside that are accessed only by modest paths.

in some remote areas, there is a natural resonant echo and unexplained presences.

17

mount hood with its whiten cone, is an anchor for the city. it can be seen most days, seemingly, floating in the air. long time residents point to it reliably in the east.

in contrast mount st. helens with its flat top and noted for its rare appearances, causes everyone to look alertly to the northeast north.

18

expect morning fog and light showers today, one forecaster might cite. fog to fade by mid day and showers to lighten by the afternoon, all to be replaced by part clouds part sun and part diminished sky.

expect seasonal humidity and little variance in temperatures or temperaments.

19

walking in the pearl district; amidst the renewal of lofts & warehouses and the creation of new slender urban parks and the new city regulations; time is everywhere. it is simultaneously morning and afternoon.

it is polished gray before sunset and it rains optimism and everyone expects it.

20

on morrison street, before the bridge that bridges to downtown, is the masonic temple and the drama theatre, on the same block, directly across from each other. the other buildings on that block take on the same stateliness. people walk evenly. dogs bark calmly. in the entrances of apartment houses, are the soft doors.

there is a woman who walks down the street, in step to its pitch and a man, who walks backwards, up the street, in hopes of slowing time.

§

constructions

look for the ceiling

i

look for the ceiling but see a sky instead, with concrete clouds ..
rectangular clouds in a geometric dome forming a half cylindered tunnel
in the underground ..

the descent into the underground is by way of broad formal stairs,
several levels .. people move quickly up & down the stairwells .. the
main floor opens unto a concrete cavern revealing additional layers;
platforms, stairs, tracks & trains; trains stationary & trains in transit ..
tickets are available by machine or by the central kiosk which is peopled
.. green line red line & blue; follow the broad painted arrows & study
the sensibly planted maps as while walking to the primary platform for
waiting ..

•

is little

the space in an afternoon;

while waiting a train

.. not very wide

that has been carved out

though quite deep

and crevices

.. filled with striking knots

ii

there is music in the tunnels, a combination of metallic wind, the shrill voices of a narrator over head; the conversation of all of us, who are waiting .. public art, murals & ads require a short attention span as a multi-car train slides to a halt .. metro riders surge as one force unto the waiting train cars, whilst an equivalent force surge outward .. everyone settles inside & doors close .. inside everyone settles, closing doors .. the train escalates from white light into the black ..

•

你
 you are that,
 someone could point,
 pointing to the platform
 pointing to the crowds
  we are
  the parts
  of the sum ..
  humanity moving
  by rail

iii

    we avoid looking directly at our neighbor in front of us or next to us .. we are bodies & thought moving thru space; space bathed by clear light & darkened light alternately .. and as we emerge from the tunnels; further along the green line red line & blue; we see the city dismembered .. half a city block, there, in one glimpse; three people conversing on a ornate balcony, over here, & in another instance; a sharp yellow blot of sun in day, a pale yellow blot of moon in night.

•

find a house ..
a blockish home

notice
the sifting light
in the background
    observe sounds & brightnesses

    freeze the moment
    and move on ..

one stop for three; one, two & three; minutes, an animated painting of a tree-lined tidy street, a slum, a famous street, a waiting restaurant; or a school, a church, a factory scene, a cemetery scene .. a few people, multitudes of persons will enter or exit .. multitudes of persons, a few people, will exit or enter .. someone holds their breath for five; one, two, three, four & five, seconds as the train car doors close .. we move to the next stop & the next; avenida placer, plaza de armas, the east bay; 1st street, 99th avenue; or la zona rosa ..distances collapse & distances are later to expand .. each stop is a expressive announcement of a place we could want to know ..

•

to pause,
for a moment,
only to revive
yourself ..

the train doors are lungs
open close
inhale exhale

V

the moving cell is populated by 40 or 50 or more people and, as is, the next movable cell & another .. everyone enters & exits with determined reserve; from or to home, work or the market .. the sound of people talking, the brush of bodies moving about, doors opening doors closing, trains slowing down trains accelerating & the invisible narrator over head ..

we can see the perfect face in a mass of 100 people & we can distinguish the perfect voice in a crowd of 100 people, but only for a moment ..

•

to stumble,

thru a crowd

of standing

patient people,

is to comprehend

from a exceptional position

vi

we arrive to a platform inside the underground in a sterilized light ..

we arrive to a platform brightened outside in daylight filtered thru trees, blocked by tall buildings, obscured by a stadium ..

we arrive to a platform darkened outside when it is night & calm or night & unsettled .. then walking briskly to the university, the club, the house of a relations .. strolling absently to the mall, the dentist, the home of the friend .. to the dentist, the mall, the home of the friend absently strolling ..

•

the mind plays a game

it blots out present direct experience
if you concentrate on the imagination

but for how many lost exquisite moments?
before your attention
becomes the direct experience
present again ..

study the sensibly planted maps as while walking to the primary platform for waiting .. look for the ceiling but see a sky instead, with concrete clouds .. follow the broad painted arrows .. rectangular clouds in a geometric dome forming a half cylindered tunnel in the underground .. people move quickly up & down the stairwells .. the main floor opens unto a cavern concrete revealing additional layers; platforms, stairs, tracks & trains; the descent into the underground is by way of broad formal stairs, several levels .. tickets are available by the central kiosk which is peopled or by machine..

trains stationary & trains in transit .. green line red line & blue ..

•

ropes of sounds, & its associative scenes

in the metro ..

deconstructed into pieces

and then reconstructed ..

recently made blocks of noise

blocks of images

forming new resonance ..

wet thick knots

damp broad gels

of montage --

and other forms of fleeting juxtaposition

◆

i

the highways curve in to the air here
in the morning coarse air
     with imperfections of dust in it
and what surrounds us, we so clearly see --
it is the uncomplicated series of exchanges
     to anywhere

ii

in october, its last day, we walk a farm road that is frequented by birds anticipating winter .. i am tall although, at times, you are taller .. this place is dominated by small waterways & preferred by those pre-wintered birds: those geese, ducks, cranes & divine herons .. and we navigate the bridge the path the pathless, the width of the day .. i am wise nevertheless, sometimes, you are wiser .. there are small turtles, little benign snakes, tiny fish swimming near us .. there are birds in flight & stealth crouching creatures near us .. i am light however, frequently, you are pure light .. at the edge of an overlook is the best moment, frozen with marvel we survey the whole of this setting .. every pocket of land, brush, & small trees .. every pocket of marsh, shallow green aquatics & channels .. a farm road .. and the whole of this setting ..

iii

spiral
spiral sky,
with its ceiling lifted
turns away from us,
has a synchronous hue

although hills
with an irrational glow
bleed & spread at its edges

one summer, we stay in a house that crackles up a hill .. it has a long steady deep descending narrow deep ascending corridor of stairs .. you have straightened your hair, i contemplate shaving .. there are distant journeys in the evening .. you carry a sketch book .. so, one september, we stay in a victorian near the city gardens .. it has three floors & a basement although we prefer only one introverted room .. you have cut your hair, i start shaving .. there are liquid strolls in the nearby community grounds .. you carry a map of the area .. and one weekend, we stay in a miniscule hotel near quite a rocky seaside .. it has pathways leading west to stony coves & undulating coastlines, foggy .. you tighten your hair into a cap, i forget to shave .. there are absentminded meanderings in the midday .. you carry a clarity in your eyes .. likewise, one day, we stay in a downtown apartment hotel close to a public hall & postal organizations .. it has an elevator but we frequent the stairs .. you are growing your hair, i have switched to an electric razor .. there is a milky walk in the stainless morning .. you carry a paper, paper, note pad paper

V

several streets converge in this chaotic, *correction* quixotic, part of town that is nearby a subsequent courtyard & its vicinity, in an elder district in the hills .. this could be an abandoned courtyard, just as it is, for us .. trees, thick branches, protracted leaves amid brick linings: a small number of non-used buildings, a few elements of seating, an open pebbled floor .. and more - several views congregate with extended sights of an eventual sea & its surroundings .. this might be an abandoned sea, left as it is, for us .. a city, a harbor & its bay .. marching waves & oscillating winds, oscillating sea birds, a sky grey brittle .. a navy departing & a navy arriving ..

vi

is it that we are clay designed to be plastered about(?) .. these rooms: the substances of walls .. and we are plastered about because we insist on becoming stretched .. and between us this knowledge .. there is an expansion an expression in to the ingredients of paint .. we are solvents, pigments & oil covering rectangular surfaces, reassigning space & texture .. the air particles, the atmosphere circulates pressure & temperature .. this is part of it .. so regulates exchanges of oxygen & moisture; the freshening of surfaces .. we are part of it

how is it that we know(?) .. we feel as floor; of glue, nail, sealant & the length & width of wooden plank .. these rooms .. the texture the pattern of wooden plank is solid precise perfect ideal solid complete .. the formula of entries & passageways .. and these theories between us .. we make possible flow & transition .. structured space .. we create flow & transition .. deliberated openings .. and the light passes painless thru panes, windows .. this is it .. sand, soda ash, limestone .. we are it .. the human rooms .. wood, cut-glass & metallics

THANKS

anne valley-fox

barbara rockman

barbara rishel

camille gibeault

cara olson-kolb

gladys yolanda padilla

hannah thein

janet waltz

jean mackenzie johnson

laurie mitchell

nancy brown

penny plautz

ranjit khalsa

sarrih pavel

theus

"i am a distracted child" by juan ramón jiménez
eternidades (1917)